DISNEY'S

chicken little

The Essential Guide

A big pig with
a big heart

This fish has plenty
to say for himself

An agony aunt
in the making

Town hero or
scaremonger?

Written by
Catherine Saunders

Disney's

chicken little

The Essential Guide

Contents

Chicken Little

O ne fateful day a year ago, something fell on Chicken Little's head. How was he to know it was just a stupid little acorn? He naturally thought the sky was falling! If only he could turn back the clock...

"The sky is falling!"

Talk of the town

Chicken Little made one little mistake and no one will let him forget it. First there was a book, then a book on tape, then a board game, then spoons, plates, and a website, and now they want to make a film about him! Will the people of Oakey Oaks ever give him a break and let him lead a normal life?

Proud red comb

Cool green glasses

Funky green t-shirt

Chicken Little really believed that he was saving the town—but even a year later he is still laughed at wherever he goes. What hurts him most of all is that his dad, Buck, didn't believe him. He even called him "crazy" on live TV!

Tiny tail

Small chicken feet

Likes

 Likes Chilling out with his best buddies, Abby, Runt, and Fish.

 Likes Playing baseball—he dreams of being a star, just like his dad.

 Dislikes Talking about his problems—he would rather just ignore them!

 Dislikes Being stared at and made fun of wherever he goes. Why can't people just leave him alone?

Dislikes

Cluck house

Behind this normal-looking front door lives Oakey Oaks' most infamous resident—Chicken Little. When Chicken Little wants to escape from his problems he hangs out in his bedroom. He little expects that this safe place will soon be the scene of some strange goings on.

Good friends

Chicken Little has three great buddies whom he can always count on. Abby, Runt, and Fish also know what it is like to feel like misfits. Together they are going to show Oakey Oaks that it is OK to be different.

Little

Chicken Little's all-time hero is his dad, Buck. He would love to be strong and tough, just like him. When Buck Cluck talks, folks sit up and take notice!

Fact

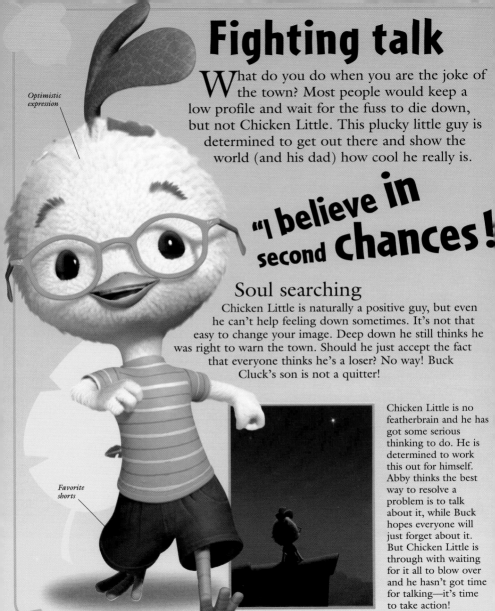

Fighting talk

What do you do when you are the joke of the town? Most people would keep a low profile and wait for the fuss to die down, but not Chicken Little. This plucky little guy is determined to get out there and show the world (and his dad) how cool he really is.

Optimistic expression

"I believe in second chances!"

Soul searching

Chicken Little is naturally a positive guy, but even he can't help feeling down sometimes. It's not that easy to change your image. Deep down he still thinks he was right to warn the town. Should he just accept the fact that everyone thinks he's a loser? No way! Buck Cluck's son is not a quitter!

Favorite shorts

Chicken Little is no featherbrain and he has got some serious thinking to do. He is determined to work this out for himself. Abby thinks the best way to resolve a problem is to talk about it, while Buck hopes everyone will just forget about it. But Chicken Little is through with waiting for it all to blow over and he hasn't got time for talking—it's time to take action!

8

A fine mess

Some folks just seem to attract trouble! When Chicken Little has an encounter with a vicious enemy—chewing gum on the sidewalk—the sticky situation goes from bad to worse. As Chicken Little tries to free himself from the gum, his pants fall off! What a way to start the school day!

Big ideas

He may be smaller than average but Chicken Little has some big ideas. He knows in his heart that he can be a hero; he just needs a chance to prove it. Chicken Little has come up with a foolproof plan—he is going to become a baseball star, just like his dad. But he doesn't plan on having to deal with some visitors from outer space.

Buck Cluck

It's not easy being a lone parent but Buck Cluck gives it his best shot. He loves his son more than anything and can't bear to see him being laughed at. Buck feels he's to blame for Chicken Little's problems but doesn't know how to make things right.

Proud red comb, just like Chicken Little's!

"Just try not to get your hopes too high"

Thinning tail feathers

Regular guy

These days Buck is a stressed-out dad. Keeping Chicken Little out of trouble is a full-time job!

Straining waistband

Chicken legs

Buck was a big baseball hero at high school. He won every trophy going and was the coolest rooster in class.

Likes — Popcorn. You could say Buck is a (pop)corn-fed chicken!

Likes — A good game of baseball, with his son on the winning team.

Dislikes — Emotional scenes. Buck is a guy's guy.

Dislikes — Letting his son down. He loves that little guy more than anything.

Abby is spot on when she says that Buck and Chicken Little don't talk enough. They are typical stubborn roosters—ashamed to talk about their feelings. If only Chicken Little realized how much his dad loves him and if only Buck understood how much his son looks up to him. What a pair of birdbrains!

Buck's face says it all. Chicken Little is just going to embarrass him—again!

Buck

Buck used to have the body of an Olympic athlete—but these days he is twice the man he used to be. He says he just has thick feathers.

Fact

Father and son

When Buck looks at Chicken Little he sees a small guy with a big heart. He would give anything to make the last year disappear. When Chicken Little reveals that he wants to play baseball, Buck tries to be a supportive dad. Secretly, he thinks that Chicken Little would be more suited to chess club. But this time, Chicken Little is going to prove his dad wrong!

Abby Mallard

Abby Mallard pretends that it doesn't hurt when people call her "The Ugly Duckling." Deep down she would love to be a graceful swan. But with her kind heart and clever brain, her friends can see that Abby is truly beautiful on the inside.

"Stop the squawk and try the talk!"

Problems solved

Underneath her sassy exterior, Abby is a real romantic. She believes that the answer to any problem can be found with the right teen magazine quiz.

Strong teeth

Extra-long neck

Abby

When people tease her, Abby's attitude is "Who cares what they think? Just let it roll off your back!"

Fact

Large, webbed feet

What do you get when you cross a duck with a pig? A great singing duo, that's what! For once, Abby unruffles her feathers and gets down to some karaoke.

If only he would notice me!

But I'm just his best friend!

Secret crush

Abby is secretly in love with a member of the gang. She thinks he is brave and kind and totally misunderstood. But this little guy has no idea at all about Abby's true feelings. However, the teen magazines say that the best relationships are based on true friendship, so maybe one day she will get her chicken.

Abby usually has a cool head under pressure—but when she is faced with aliens from outer space her calm facade starts to "quack."

For once Abby is lost for words. Her magazines have not prepared her for dealing with an alien invasion!

Likes

 Likes Romantic movies, especially chick flicks.

 Likes A certain, smaller-than-average chicken (mentioning no names, of course!)

 Dislikes Foxy Loxy—she gave Abby her nickname and now the whole town calls her "The Ugly Duckling."

 Dislikes People who can't talk about their feelings.

Dislikes

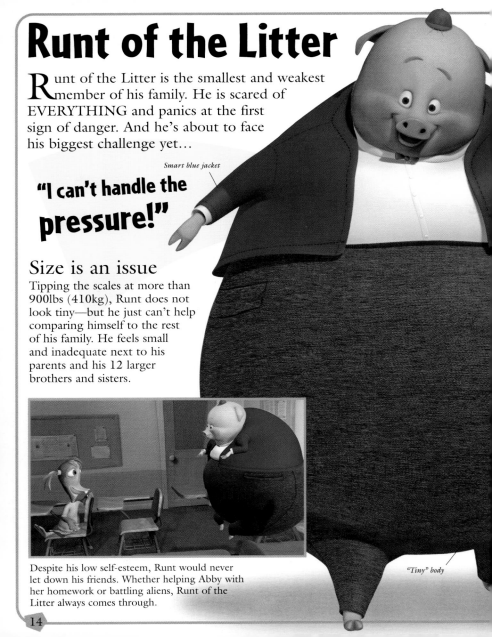

Runt of the Litter

Runt of the Litter is the smallest and weakest member of his family. He is scared of EVERYTHING and panics at the first sign of danger. And he's about to face his biggest challenge yet…

Smart blue jacket

"I can't handle the pressure!"

Size is an issue

Tipping the scales at more than 900lbs (410kg), Runt does not look tiny—but he just can't help comparing himself to the rest of his family. He feels small and inadequate next to his parents and his 12 larger brothers and sisters.

"Tiny" body

Despite his low self-esteem, Runt would never let down his friends. Whether helping Abby with her homework or battling aliens, Runt of the Litter always comes through.

Likes

 Likes Dressing smartly—it makes him feel good.

 Likes Listening to music—his favorites are disco divas.

 Dislikes Scary situations, especially ones involving aliens. Yikes!

 Dislikes Gym class and any kind of sport. Runt is not a natural athlete.

Dislikes

Hidden depths

Runt knows that he is a natural-born worrier with a tendency to freak out at the first sign of trouble. Whenever he finds himself in a scary situation, he sings. It makes him feel calmer and helps him to be brave in the face of danger.

Runt feels the pressure

Runt

Runt's oldest brother weighs 1200lbs (545kg.) The secrets of his success are doughnuts, French fries, and triple-chocolate fudge sundaes. Runt has got a lot to learn!

Fact

If singing fails, Runt has a back-up plan. He always keeps a brown paper bag or two in his jacket pocket. As soon as Runt starts to panic, he breathes into the bag. It really works, but let's just say that he gets through a lot of bags!

Fish out of Water

In every class there's always one kid who stands out from the crowd. In Chicken Little's school, it is Fish out of Water. He may not say very much but he is not afraid to be different!

"Glub!"

Fun guy
Fish out of Water is not a regular marine creature. For a start, he lives in Oakey Oaks, not the ocean—and he walks rather than swims! Only his friends Chicken Little, Abby, and Runt can understand him when he talks. To everyone else it just sounds like "Glub!"

Special water filled helmet

Permanently cheerful expression

Fins adapted to work like arms

Tail fins work like feet

Fish is a true friend. When his pal Chicken Little decides he is going to be a baseball star, Fish is right behind him. Go Acorns! Fish is suddenly the team's biggest fan.

Fish
Fish's family moved to Oakey Oaks as part of an exchange program. His parents are top scientists and they want to see what life is like outside the ocean.

Fact

16

Likes

 Likes Challenges—Fish loves exploring new things!

 Likes Chatting—Fish is a real talker, it's just that few people can understand him!

 Dislikes Swimming—Fish thinks his tail was made for walking not swimming!

 Dislikes People who upset his friends—that makes him really mad!

Dislikes

Fish and Runt couldn't be more different. One isn't afraid of anything, while the other is scared of his own shadow! But they have one important thing in common—friendship. They can always rely on each other for support.

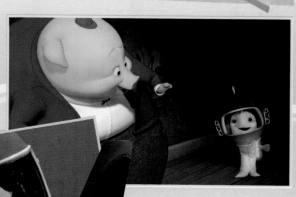

What's this? Only Fish really wants to know...

Naturally curious

Sometimes Fish just can't help himself. If he sees anything unusual or interesting he has to investigate. One day his natural curiosity is going to land him in trouble, or at least give Runt a nervous breakdown!

Foxy Loxy

Some folk just seem to have it all—looks, brains, athletic ability, popularity. But Foxy Loxy also has a mean streak. Her favorite pastime is making Chicken Little's life as miserable as possible.

"Present, pretty, and punctual"

The real Foxy

To most of the folks in Oakey Oaks, Foxy Loxy is a model citizen—but Chicken Little knows her true character. Somehow she always manages to get him into trouble and make him look stupid. It's time for someone to teach her a lesson!

Pretty pigtails

Don't be deceived by this sweet expression

Ladylike pose

Foxes have always picked on chickens. Just what is their problem? Chicken Little thinks that Foxy might need anger-management therapy to help beat her chicken-hating issues.

Baseball star

Foxy Loxy is the star player of the Oakey Oaks Acorns baseball team. Thanks to her, the Acorns are enjoying their best season since Buck Cluck was a player—and Foxy makes sure the whole town knows it! Foxy thinks it's hilarious when Chicken Little decides he, too, wants to play baseball. She can't wait to help him fail!

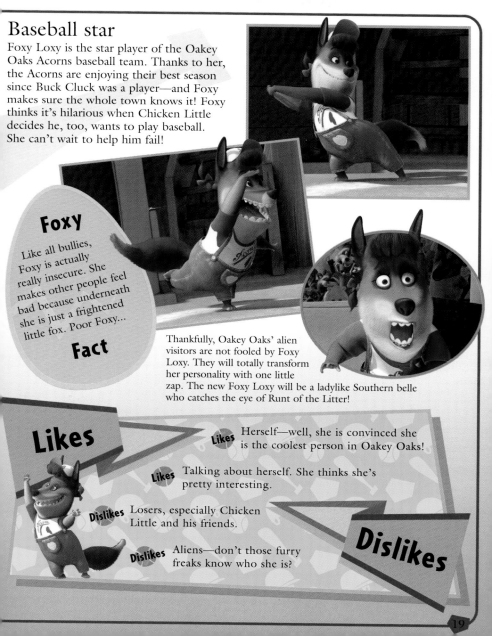

Foxy Fact

Like all bullies, Foxy is actually really insecure. She makes other people feel bad because underneath she is just a frightened little fox. Poor Foxy...

Thankfully, Oakey Oaks' alien visitors are not fooled by Foxy Loxy. They will totally transform her personality with one little zap. The new Foxy Loxy will be a ladylike Southern belle who catches the eye of Runt of the Litter!

Likes

Likes Herself—well, she is convinced she is the coolest person in Oakey Oaks!

Likes Talking about herself. She thinks she's pretty interesting.

Dislikes Losers, especially Chicken Little and his friends.

Dislikes Aliens—don't those furry freaks know who she is?

Dislikes

19

School

A t first glance Oakey Oaks looks like a sleepy little town where nothing much happens. But, in reality, it's a crazy place where anything is possible! From alien invasions to smash-hit movies, Oakey Oaks has seen it all.

Main entrance

School bell

Principal's office

School bus

OAKEY OAKS

The school bell

Oakey Oaks Middle School stands at the center of the town. When aliens strike, ringing the school bell is the perfect way for Chicken Little to alert the townsfolk. Next time, of course, he will make sure that the aliens stick around so he doesn't look like a loser! Again.

Chicken Little's classroom

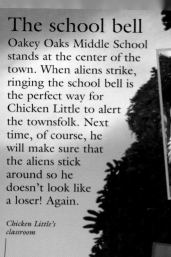

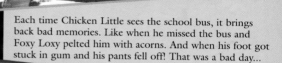

Each time Chicken Little sees the school bus, it brings back bad memories. Like when he missed the bus and Foxy Loxy pelted him with acorns. And when his foot got stuck in gum and his pants fell off! That was a bad day...

Oakey

Oakey Oaks Middle School is famous for some high-achieving ex-students. Bull Gates, Moolia Roberts, and Pig Diddy learnt everything they know here!

Fact

School lockers

Being smaller than average makes life difficult for Chicken Little. Even his locker is on the top row, which makes it too high for him to reach. But that doesn't stop our plucky hero from finding clever ways to propel himself up there. He's a resourceful little guy! All he needs is a shoelace and a window shade!

Classmates

Oakey Oaks is a pretty regular school. The students learn all the usual subjects—mutton, pigonometry, fishstory, duckology, henglish, and cowculus.

Goosey Loosey

Every bully needs a sidekick and Foxy Loxy has Goosey Loosey. She is not the brainiest bird in school, but Foxy picked her because she does whatever Foxy tells her! Goosey says little and lets Foxy do all the talking.

Girly red dress

Big, clumsy feet

While Foxy verbally abuses Chicken Little, Goosey Loosey supplies the muscle. She takes great delight in doing a lot more than ruffling his feathers—in front of the whole class!

Class Register

Foxy Loxy
Goosey Loosey
Runt of the Litter
Henny Penny
Ducky Lucky
Fuzzy Wuzzy
Morkubine Porcupine
Fish out of Water
Abby Mallard
Chicken Little

Goosy Loosey lands Chicken Little in yet more trouble when the unlucky guy sets off the fire alarm by accident. He's starting to think seriously about the benefits of home school!

Class

Oakey Oaks Middle School is well known for its dodgeball and baseball teams. Chicken Little and his friends are usually happier to watch than to compete!

Fact

Gym class

The gym teacher believes that gym class should be as tough as possible. For a game of dodgeball he splits the class into two teams—popular kids versus unpopular kids. Guess which team Chicken Little, Abby, Runt, and Fish are on?

Dodgeball games provide Foxy Loxy with perfect opportunities to humiliate less athletic kids.

Heads up

Morkubine Porcupine uses his head in the classroom, but he has problems on the dodgeball court— the ball often gets stuck on his spines!

Mr. Woolensworth

Chicken Little's teacher is a wise old sheep who has been teaching at the school for as long as anyone can remember. He firmly believes that every student should be fluent in mutton.

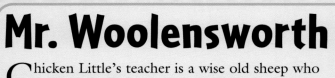

Roll call

Every morning Mr. Woolensworth takes a roll call of his students. Once again he has to give Chicken Little a tardy. One more and Chicken Little will be in detention. If only Mr. Woolensworth knew what the poor little guy had to go through just to get to school, he might be a little more sympathetic!

Fine head of wool

Mr. Woolensworth has had a long and distinguished career. He has taught everyone, from Mayor Lurkey to Buck Cluck, during his time at Oakey Oaks Middle School.

"He's been nothing but trouble!"

Roll call register

As the class settles down to their first lesson, Abby tries not to worry about the empty desk behind her. Where can Chicken Little have got to? With his ability to attract trouble, he could be anywhere!

Turkey Lurkey

Tall, grand-looking hat

Mr. Mayor

Turkey Lurkey wants the whole world to know how powerful and influential he is. Wherever he goes he makes sure that he gets noticed. At baseball matches he sits in a private box festooned with brightly colored bunting, just so that everyone knows he's there.

Mayor Turkey Lurkey is the most important guy in town—or at least he thinks he is. He is about to serve a record seventh term, but only because no one else wants the job!

"Not that pipsqueak!"

When faced with what looks like a full-scale alien invasion, Mayor Lurkey shows his true colors. He surrenders immediately rather than making a stand and trying to save the town.

Fancy rosette

Baseball

Oakey Oaks hasn't had a baseball team to be proud of since Buck Cluck was the star player 20 years ago. However, with the unstoppable Foxy Loxy leading the way, the Acorns are now just one game away from glory.

Go Acorns! The Acorns mascot makes sure that the crowd is fully behind the team as they bid to bring glory back to Oakey Oaks.

Old rivals

It is the most important game in Oakey Oaks for years. The Acorns are facing their old rivals, the Spud Valley Taters. But with Foxy Loxy in the team, the Acorns are looking like an outfit to be reckoned with!

The Taters' star player is their pitcher. He's a long-legged stork with a strong arm.

What's the score?

Abby and Runt like to keep busy. They may not be the greatest athletes in the world but they can still help out the team by keeping score. Let's hope the Acorns can make them proud!

Tension mounts

The announcer makes sure the crowd knows exactly what's happening during the match. He's supposed to be unbiased but of course he's rooting for the Acorns!

Taters baseball cap

Grunts as he pitches

Mayor Lurkey really wants the Acorns to beat the Taters. He would love to have something to gobble about and make him feel even more important. Maybe next season he will get a bigger box with even more fancy bunting!

Town pride

The Acorns haven't beaten the Taters for 20 years—so the whole town's pride rests on this one match. No pressure on the team, then!

Batter up!

The Acorns have a serious problem. Three of their best players are out of action for the crucial game. There is only one player the coach can call on— Chicken Little. The little guy's big moment has finally arrived.

Time to be a hero!

As he steps up to the plate, Chicken Little can hardly believe what's happening. Abby, Runt, and Fish have confidence in their friend, even if the rest of the town think he is going to fail. Go, Chicken Little!

Chicken Little has waited a long time for a chance to prove he can be a winner. He has trained hard and this time he is determined to be a success.

Sports

Oakey Oaks' other favorite sports are stable tennis, moodo, crowquet, and cross-country flying.

Fact

28

Loser!

Everyone in the crowd is sure that Chicken Little is going to fail and become the joke of the town again. What an embarrassment! But the little guy is determined to prove every single one of them wrong!

The baseball bat is twice as big as Chicken Little. It is so heavy that he can hardly lift it, let alone hit the ball. It's time to show the world that size doesn't matter—it's what's inside that counts!

The pride of Oakey Oaks rests on Chicken Little's tiny shoulders.

Strike two!

Chicken Little's nerves seem to be getting the better of him. He misses the first two pitches and the crowd begins to turn ugly. Buck is too nervous to watch his son. He is terrified that Chicken Little will feel even worse than he did before! The Taters think they have already won the game. They are totally confident that Chicken Little will miss the final pitch and that the Acorns' long-time losing streak will continue for another year.

Bat is heavier than Chicken Little!

Tiny chicken feet take the weight.

Home run

Chicken Little has one more chance to hit the ball and prove to Oakey Oaks that he is not a loser. If he misses, he may as well pack up and leave town for good. Surely he deserves a lucky break.

Chicken Little hits the ball so hard that he falls and lands in his helmet!

This fielder is shocked

The pitcher is stunned

It's a hit!

The crowd can hardly believe their eyes— Chicken Little has hit the ball! All he has to do now is run. Sounds simple, but unfortunately Chicken Little has never actually hit the ball before and doesn't even know which way to run!

Chicken Little finally runs in the right direction and is determined to go all the way. But it's a close ca

One for the Acorns!

He's in! Chicken Little has scored a home run and won the game for the Acorns! Mayor Lurkey and the folk of Oakey Oaks can hold their heads up high. They have beaten the Spud Valley Taters at last, and what's more the hero of the day is a smaller-than-average guy called Chicken Little!

Chicken Little has never felt this good before!

This fielder is overwhelmed

This fielder can hardly believe his eyes!

Abby and Runt are delighted for their friend. It looks like his problems are over and he can get on with his new life, as a hero!

Chicken Little's friends celebrate by soaking him with the team drink. He was the last player in but now he's the coolest member of the team!

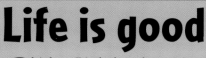

Life is good

Chicken Little is carried shoulder high by his teammates. He is an even bigger star than Foxy Loxy now! Runt, Fish, and Abby are so proud of him—they always knew he could do it.

Chicken Little has done it! He has gone from zero to hero with one mighty swipe of his bat. The last year has finally been forgotten and Oakey Oaks loves him.

Hero!

Chicken Little has shown that a little faith in yourself can go a long way! He refused to give up when most people thought he would just make a fool of himself. Of course, he always had the support of his friends.

Chicken Little struts with the confident stride of a winner!

"I am the champion!"

Buck is so proud of his son. At times he didn't think the boy could do it but Chicken Little has shown him that he is one tough little guy. Life can finally start getting back to normal.

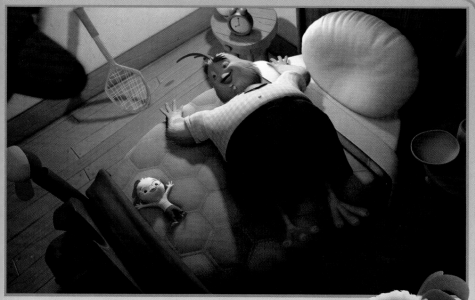

Father and son

Buck and Chicken Little feel really great after
the baseball game—but if Abby were there
she would tell them that they still have a lot
of "issues" to work through. Chicken Little
considers talking to his dad about how difficult
things have been lately but he decides that
this moment is too good to spoil.

*Chicken Little
rocks the
Cluck house!*

Chicken Little is so
happy that he can't
help singing!
Maybe he should
get together with
Abby and Runt and
form a super-cool
rock band! On
second thoughts,
maybe not...

Chicken Little has never been
happier in his entire life. He
knows that the baseball game
has turned things around for
him. He is never ever going
to be a loser again.

*At this point in
time, life is good!*

33

Here we go again!

Just when Chicken Little thought he had finally turned his life around, a strange discovery turns his world upside down—again. Why do these weird things always happen to him?

As Chicken Little gazes out of the window to thank his lucky stars, something strange happens. Is it just his imagination or is that shining star getting bigger and bigger?

Not only is the star getting bigger, it is heading straight for Chicken Little! The next thing he knows, he is on the other side of his bedroom with a bump on his head!

Weird alien circuitry

S.O.S.

Although Chicken Little tries to ignore it, this time it looks like a piece of the sky really has fallen on him. There is no way he can handle a serious situation like this alone. He needs help to figure out what to do but he can't tell his dad. Things have just got so good between them and this sky business could ruin everything!

What's this?

Chicken Little can't even begin to imagine what all those wires are for. Whatever it is, he is pretty sure that it is going to create a problem!

On closer inspection, it seems that the mysterious piece of sky is some kind of invisible panel. Chicken Little sees his reflection in it, but this is no ordinary reflection!

Chicken Little decides to call for backup—Abby, Runt, and Fish, of course. Chicken Little knows that they will help him.

They're here!

Abby and the gang rush straight to Chicken Little's house as soon as they can. Abby is sure that there is a logical explanation, but the friends are baffled. What on earth could this thing be?

Abby leaps into action the minute she gets Chicken Little's call.

35

Kidnapped!

Chicken Little can usually count on his friends. But this time things are about to get out of hand. Can a smaller-than-average chicken, a love-struck duck, a pig with size issues, and a kooky fish really handle an alien invasion on their own?

Flying Fish

Fish's curious nature gets him into real trouble this time! While the others try to come up with a plan, Fish takes a closer look at the alien panel. He presses a few buttons—and goes for the ride of his life. The only problem is, there don't seem to be any brakes!

All the gang can see of Fish is his glowing stick disappearing across the sky. Chicken Little, Abby, and Runt are determined to follow him and save their kidnapped friend from whatever the aliens might have in store for him.

Landing site

The gang follow Fish to the baseball field. Just a few hours ago, the field was the scene of Chicken Little's greatest triumph—but now its like alien central! All the friends want to do is run in the opposite direction, but Fish needs them and they can't let their friend down.

The gang can hardly believe their eyes! As Runt and Chicken Little run to the dugout for safety, Abby is too terrified to move. Luckily, Chicken Little grabs her just in time.

Awesome power

The ground starts to shake and the lights start to flash. Chicken Little and the gang have no idea whether the visitors from outer space are friendly or not. What will they do to poor, helpless little Fish?

Casting an eerie glow, the huge spaceship touches down on the baseball field. The gang watch in horror as a door opens and Fish floats inside.

Saucer-shaped hull

Underside of ship is made of lots of familiar-looking panels.

Landing legs extend from beneath craft

The alien ship

The friends decide they must face their fears and investigate the alien ship if they want to save Fish. The gang watch the aliens leave the ship, so that's one less thing for them to worry about. Or is it?

Abby and Chicken Little are not really sure that they want to find out what is inside the alien ship!

Hall of horrors

The alien ship is full of unbelievably scary things. Surely those can't be eyeballs, brains, hearts, and lungs! And what is that furry thing? Did it really just wink at Chicken Little?

All this excitement is too much for sensitive Runt. He's convinced that he'll never get out alive and he can't handle the pressure. Thankfully, Abby and Chicken Little are there to calm him down.

V.I.P. guests

How often do you get a chance to meet people from outer space? It's the opportunity of a lifetime! But somehow Chicken Little and the gang don't feel like welcoming their inter-galactic visitors. They would rather run in the opposite direction!

Here's Fish

Uh-oh, it looks like the gang's too late to save Fish, after all. The aliens must have zapped him!

Aliens' main viewing portal

Scary red lights

Hull made of weird alien alloy

Powerful landing lights

Alien plans show Earth as a target!

Of course Fish is OK! It takes more than a few scary aliens to catch him.

Under attack!

The gang discover some secret plans aboard the alien ship. It looks like the aliens have been on an inter-galactic destruction spree—and Earth is next! Now they must warn the town before it's too late.

The aliens

Oakey Oaks has a serious problem! It doesn't look as if these aliens are in town for a relaxing holiday. They seem to have more serious business on their minds—like total destruction!

There are lots of scary things about these visitors from outer space, but the most frightening has to be their long tentacles. Each tentacle has something sharp and mean on the end, designed to cause maximum damage.

Antenna with built-in searchlight

Tentacle with sharp hook attachment

The chase

The aliens use their searchlights to hunt for the friends as they hide in a cornfield. They use their tentacles to chop a path toward them. Luckily, the corn stalks fall on the gang so the aliens can't see them.

It soon becomes clear that the aliens won't let anything stand in their way. Oakey Oaks had better watch out—these guys have powers that are out of this world!

Mean-looking pincers

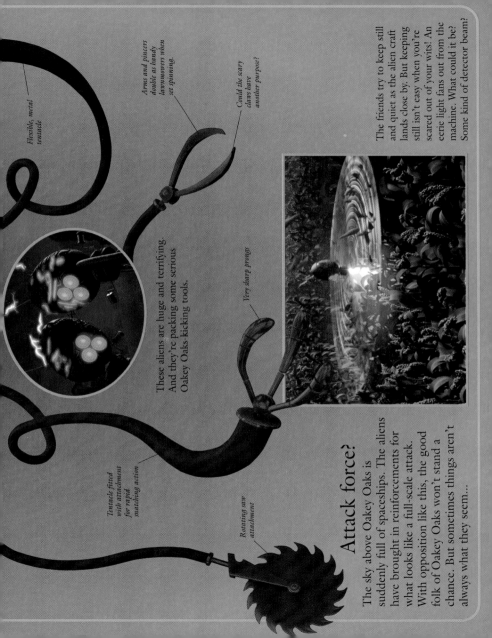

Flexible, metal tentacle

Arms and pincers double as handy lawnmowers when set spinning.

Could the scary claws have another purpose?

These aliens are huge and terrifying. And they're packing some serious Oakey Oaks-kicking tools.

Very sharp prongs

The friends try to keep still and quiet as the alien craft lands close by. But keeping still isn't easy when you're scared out of your wits! An eerie light fans out from the machine. What could it be? Some kind of detector beam?

Tentacle fitted with attachment for rapid matching action

Rotating saw attachment

Attack force?

The sky above Oakey Oaks is suddenly full of spaceships. The aliens have brought in reinforcements for what looks like a full-scale attack. With opposition like this, the good folk of Oakey Oaks won't stand a chance. But sometimes things aren't always what they seem...

The rescuers

Chicken Little and the gang have only one aim—to warn the rest of the town that the aliens are planning to destroy Earth. This is one time where being small is a good thing, because Chicken Little is so light that the fizz from a soda bottle gives him the boost he needs to reach the school bell.

They're behind you!

With the aliens in hot pursuit, Chicken Little, Abby, Runt, and Fish head for the school.... For once in his life Chicken Little can't wait to get there!

Chicken Little pulls the rope with all his strength!

While Chicken Little is warning the town, the rest of the gang have a serious alien situation on their hands. Caught in the glare of the aliens' spotlights, the friends are momentarily paralyzed by fear. Run!

Listen up!

The bell rings with a loud clang.

The whole town comes running when it hears the school bell, but by the time they arrive at the baseball field the aliens have vanished. Once again Chicken Little looks like a fool in front of everyone—and not even his dad believes him. The next day, things are worse than ever in the Cluck household. While Buck fields angry phone calls and emails from the townsfolk, Chicken Little still can't believe that his dad won't support him.

Chicken Little was right all along!

As the sky fills with alien spaceships, the town finally realizes that Chicken Little was right after all! But once again Chicken Little is one step ahead of the game. With his friends 100 per cent behind him as always, he needs some extra help. He is going to give his Dad one last chance to believe in him.

Chicken Little and the gang leap into action and, at last, Buck is on their side. While the rest of the town runs away from the aliens, Chicken Little runs toward them. He is sure he can sort everything out, without any need for the aliens to get scary.

Alien family

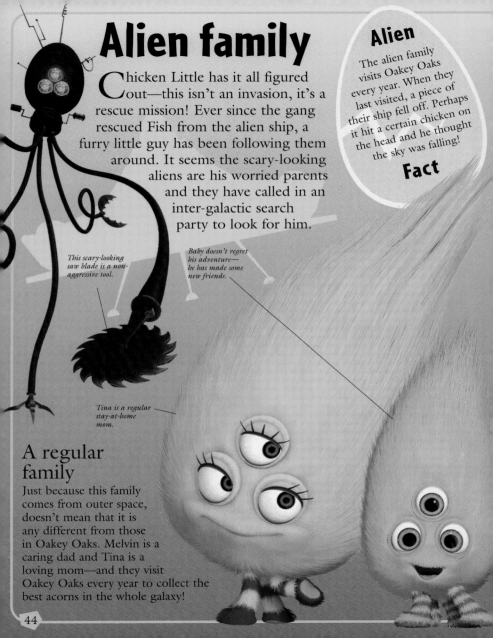

Chicken Little has it all figured out—this isn't an invasion, it's a rescue mission! Ever since the gang rescued Fish from the alien ship, a furry little guy has been following them around. It seems the scary-looking aliens are his worried parents and they have called in an inter-galactic search party to look for him.

Alien

The alien family visits Oakey Oaks every year. When they last visited, a piece of their ship fell off. Perhaps it hit a certain chicken on the head and he thought the sky was falling!

Fact

This scary-looking saw blade is a non-aggressive tool.

Baby doesn't regret his adventure—he has made some new friends.

Tina is a regular stay-at-home mom.

A regular family

Just because this family comes from outer space, doesn't mean that it is any different from those in Oakey Oaks. Melvin is a caring dad and Tina is a loving mom—and they visit Oakey Oaks every year to collect the best acorns in the whole galaxy!

Melvin is just trying to do what is right for his family.

Chicken Little realizes that the aliens are trying to find their lost child.

The alien baby didn't mean to cause a major inter-galactic incident, he just thinks that Chicken Little is the coolest guy in the whole universe. He plans to be just like his hero when he grows up!

Father and son really have worked it out this time!

A new beginning

Chicken Little and his dad are doing great, too! They have finally started talking to each other (Abby would be so proud.) They agree that they have both made mistakes and from now on father and son are going to be an unbeatable team.

A happy ending

R elax, sit back, and enjoy the story of a heroic chicken who saves the world from an alien invasion with the help of his friends—a daredevil pig, a feisty fish, and a dazzlingly beautiful duck. Sounds familiar? Sort of. Chicken Little and his friends have been given a Hollywood makeover!

Invaders From Beyond Abduct A Creature From Earth! This Creature Is Now A... FISH OUT OF WATER Watch as horror "bubbles" to the surface!

It will be the movie of the year! The whole world will sit up and take notice of Oakey Oaks, thanks to Chicken Little.

On the silver screen, Chicken Little pilots a sleek and powerful star cruiser.

My hero!

It looks like a case of life imitating art. As the dashing Chicken Little falls for Abby on the big screen, the real-life couple can't take their eyes off each other. Chicken Little has finally realized that Abby is more than just his best friend!

A little happiness

Life is very different for Chicken Little these days. He has a great relationship with his dad, he has earned the respect of the whole town, and he has the smartest girlfriend, too. But one thing has stayed the same—he still has the best friends a guy could ever want.

Movie

The producers are talking of a sequel— *Chicken Little 2: Mission to Mars.*

Fact

Runt is enjoying life more than ever—he even has his eye on a certain foxy lady.

Fish is still the same laid-back guy he always was!

"Today is a new day!"

Can life get any better for Chicken Little? He doesn't think so!

There's nothing so beautiful as a duck in love. Abby is radiant!

Chicken Little admits that the movie is slightly different from what actually happened on the day the aliens visited Oakey Oaks.... But he is just really glad that it doesn't make him look like a loser!

47

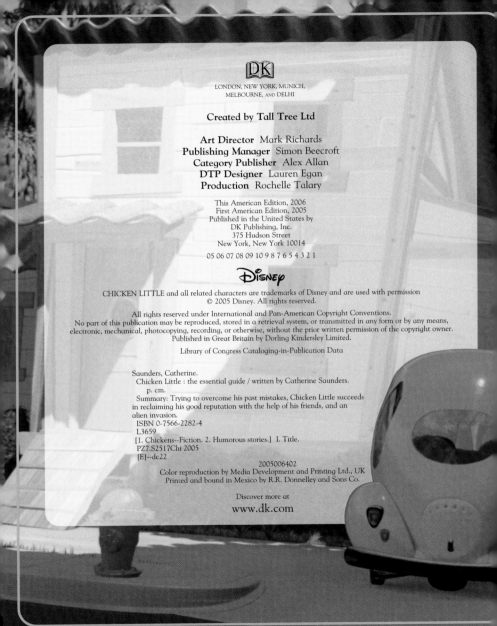

DK

LONDON, NEW YORK, MUNICH,
MELBOURNE, and DELHI

Created by Tall Tree Ltd

Art Director Mark Richards
Publishing Manager Simon Beecroft
Category Publisher Alex Allan
DTP Designer Lauren Egan
Production Rochelle Talary

This American Edition, 2006
First American Edition, 2005
Published in the United States by
DK Publishing, Inc.
375 Hudson Street
New York, New York 10014

05 06 07 08 09 10 9 8 7 6 5 4 3 2 1

Disney

Library of Congress Cataloging-in-Publication Data

Saunders, Catherine.
  Chicken Little : the essential guide / written by Catherine Saunders.
     p. cm.
  Summary: Trying to overcome his past mistakes, Chicken Little succeeds
in reclaiming his good reputation with the help of his friends, and an
alien invasion.
  ISBN 0-7566-2282-4
  L3659
  [1. Chickens--Fiction. 2. Humorous stories.] I. Title.
  PZ7.S2517Chi 2005
  [E]--dc22
                                        2005006402
Color reproduction by Media Development and Printing Ltd., UK
Printed and bound in Mexico by R.R. Donnelley and Sons Co.

Discover more at
www.dk.com